CH

D0758664

Reading & Writing

How Writing Began

Reading & Writing

How Writing Began

Marshall Cavendish
Benchmark
New York

This edition first published in 2009 in North America by Marshall Cavendish Benchmark

Marshall Cavendish Benchmark
99 White Plains Road
Tarrytown, NY 10591
www.marshallcavendish.us

Library of Congress Cataloging-in-Publication Data

Rossi, Renzo, 1940–
  How writing began / by Renzo Rossi.
    p. cm. — (Reading and writing)
  ISBN 978-0-7614-4317-9
  1. Writing—History—Juvenile literature. I. Title.
  P211.R672 2009
  411.09—dc22
                              2008032278

Text: Renzo Rossi
Editing: Cristiana Leoni
Translation: Erika Pauli
Design and layout: Luigi Ieracitano
Illustrations: Alessandro Baldanzi, Lorenzo Cecchi, Giuseppe Cicio, Sauro Giampaia,
Luigi Ieracitano, Chiara Pignaris, Paola Ravaglia, Rosanna Rea
Maps: Alessandro Bartolozzi

Printed in Malaysia
1 3 5 6 4 2

Contents

The Unwritten Word

Below: This belt is an example of *quipu*, an Incan accounting apparatus. To read it one has to know what the colors and lengths of the cords, the distance between the knots, and the number and shape of the knots all mean.

Men and women have always needed to communicate, not only directly through words and gestures, but also in a way that could cross space and time. Before the invention of writing, there were other ways of sending unwritten messages. Smoke signals could be seen at a distance, and drumbeats could be heard much farther away than a man could shout. But even these methods, like the spoken word, floated away in the air.

A way had to be found to send a message to someone far away, something that would take the place of a sound. Real objects could become symbols or stand for something else. If you give your mother a flower, you are telling her, without words, that you love her. In certain parts of Africa if a young man wanted to ask for the hand of a young woman he would send her family a cola nut. But objects could also be used as a way of storing information and handing it down to your children.

The Inca, an ancient South American civilization, kept track of the wares in their storehouses or the number of inhabitants in a region by knotting colored cords. The main problem with these unwritten words, however, was that if you didn't know the code, they were just something pretty to look at.

Above: A captain in Ghana (west Africa) commissioned this military flag in the 19th century for the day of his commission. The flag depicts a group of men holding a large fishing net. The message of the image is that the Africans have many men available to fight and conquer the European stone fort.

Right: Smoke signals can be seen miles away and were used for hundreds of years by American Indians to transmit information and warn others of danger. The method worked well—provided it was not too windy.

First Numbers, Then Words

In prehistoric times humans lived in small groups, hunting and gathering fruits, berries, and roots. At night, around the fire, they told stories or exchanged information. Sometimes they carved simple signs on stone or bone or drew figures on the walls of caves to make sure they would remember what had been said.

Then, when the first cities were founded, humans began to specialize. Some became farmers and shepherds, others learned crafts such as pottery making or weaving. Wares of one kind were produced and exchanged for other wares. They were also sent to distant places. Without written records, how were merchants and officials to keep track of what was made and sent?

Even before the written word was invented, people learned how to count. When goods were exchanged they needed some way of recording how much went out or came in. The people who first did this were the scribes, men in the service of the temple priests or the royal palace.

Opposite:
Writing began in Mesopotamia, between the Tigris and Euphrates river where the Sumerian civilization flourished during the 4th millennium BCE.

8

BLACK SEA

Troy
Hattusa
HITTITE KINGDOM
Caspian
Sea

ASSYRIA
Nineveh
Nimrod
Assur

Crete
Ugarit
Ebla
Mari
Cyprus
Byblos
MEDITERRANEAN SEA

Akkad
Kish
Nippur
SUMER
Susa
Uruk
Lagash
ELAM
Ur
Eridu

Buto
Mendes
EGYPT
Memphis
ARABIAN DESERT
Persian
Gulf

Nile

Red Sea

Below: The market of Ur, with a great stepped temple, called a *ziggurat*, in the background.

Taking Count

Writing was first created for practical reasons: for trade, recording, and accounting. The early merchants in Mesopotamia used small clay tags to indicate the quantity and quality of their wares. We might call these disk-, cone-, or sphere-shaped tags accounting tokens—a simple but revolutionary invention.

Around 3500 BCE, the tokens were enclosed in a hollow clay sphere, a sort of envelope about the size of a large orange. The signs on the tokens were also impressed on this envelope, together with the seal of the owner. It was an early step on the road to writing.

When they reached their destination, the envelopes were broken to verify the contents, thereby destroying what had been written on the outside. Eventually, it became more practical to imprint the forms of the tokens on clay tablets that, once baked, were easy to handle, easy to keep, unalterable, and almost indestructible.

Below: In Mesopotamia, clay tablets were impressed with sign that indicated the quantity of mercha dise. Lines represe one and circ represent ten.

Left: A clay envelo or *bulla*, with stam and impressed sig Next to it are som accounting tokens The conical ones r resent a small mea of grain, the spher larger measure, an the cylinders a animal.

Above: Merchants carried stone cylinder seals. They would roll the seal into fresh clay to make an imprint that acted as a signature. Some cylinder seals had intricate designs, such as the herd of cattle and row of stables on this one.

Right: Merchants delivered goods to a caravan leader, along with clay envelopes identifying the merchandise, and an ownership seal. The envelope functioned as a bill of lading, or a record, and protected the receiver from theft and fraud.

Drawing Words

In all civilizations writing began as a drawing (called a pictograph or pictogram) that represented something concrete or real: an object, an animal, a plant, a body, or a body part.

This extremely rudimentary writing system can also be read by speakers of another language. For example, today we call a drawing of an animal with widespread wings hovering in the sky a bird. The French call it *oiseau*, the Italians *uccello*, the Spanish *pájaro*, and the Germans *vogel*.

The first pictographs, however, could express only things that were real objects. Ideas such as *beauty* or *freedom*, and verbs such as *to think* or *to live* do not have a specific shape and cannot be touched.

Below: Mesopotamians us different systems fo writing and accoun ing, though there were similarities. The sign for the number 10 (*top*) resembles the pictogram for sheep or ram (*bottom*).

Left: This drawing of a fish is a decorative motif that appeared on Chinese pottery more than 6,000 years ago. It eventually became the pictogram for the word *fish*. Many pictograms can be read by people who don't know the language because they look so much like the thing they represent.

pictogram is a relatively faithful drawing of an object.
ometimes the original object is simplified and becomes more
stract, but the basic principle of pictographic writing is that
word is indicated by a recognizable picture.

ve: The pictograms in several ancient writing systems are easily
ntifiable. a) *Sun* in ancient Chinese; b) *moon* in ancient Egyptian;
ountain in Sumerian; d) *bird* in Sumerian; and f) *eye* in Cretan.

Writing in Sumeria

As in other civilizations, pictographs were the first stage in Sumerian writing. Every sign corresponded to a word.

When properly combined, repeated, or merged, these signs began to form a discourse, a simple memory aid. The pictographs became a true alphabet only when each of them was associated with a sound.

The scribes etched the outlines of the things they wanted to keep note of with a sharp instrument, or stylus, on clay tablets. In the middle of the 4th millennium BCE, these signs were standardized. The same shape would always be used to indicate a specific word, thereby ensuring that the sign would always be interpreted in the same way.

Below: Today we know the meanings of approximately 300 Sumerian pictographs. Unlike Chinese and Egypt pictographs, very few of them showe human gestures, which meant that t meaning of each written sign could not be modified. For example, addi movement to the pictograph for leg would not change its meaning to "walking," "going, or "coming."

bird   fish   donkey   ox   sun/day

wheat   orchard   plough   boomerang   foot

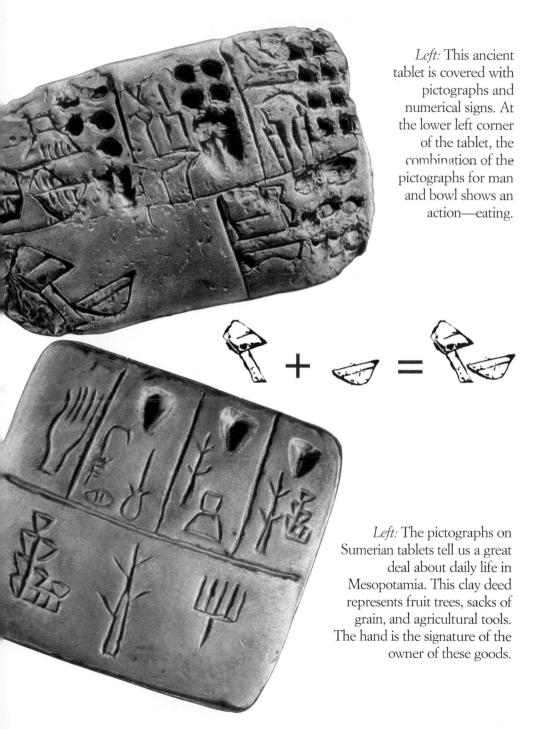

Left: This ancient tablet is covered with pictographs and numerical signs. At the lower left corner of the tablet, the combination of the pictographs for man and bowl shows an action—eating.

Left: The pictographs on Sumerian tablets tell us a great deal about daily life in Mesopotamia. This clay deed represents fruit trees, sacks of grain, and agricultural tools. The hand is the signature of the owner of these goods.

15

A Better Way to Write

It is not easy to draw a realistic plough, fish, or ox on clay. The lines vary in thickness and tend to be uneven. The Sumerians hit upon a new method. Instead of drawing lines, they used a stick with shaped ends to press signs into the clay. Curved lines gave way to straight lines, which had a vaguely triangular or wedge shape. In Latin the word for "wedge" is *cuneus*, so we called this writing cuneiform.

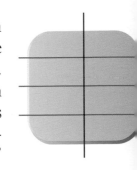

But there were other changes, too. After 2600 BCE pictographs were rotated 90 degrees; Sumerians now read horizontally, not vertically. Over time, the signs were schematized until they no longer resembled the objects they once had represented.

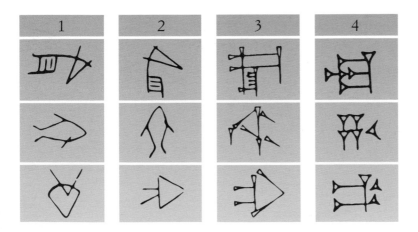

1	2	3	4

Left: 1. The primiti pictographs of a plough, a fish, and an ox

2. The pictographs rotated 90 degrees the left

3 and 4. Cuneiforn characters for the words *plough, fish,* and *ox*

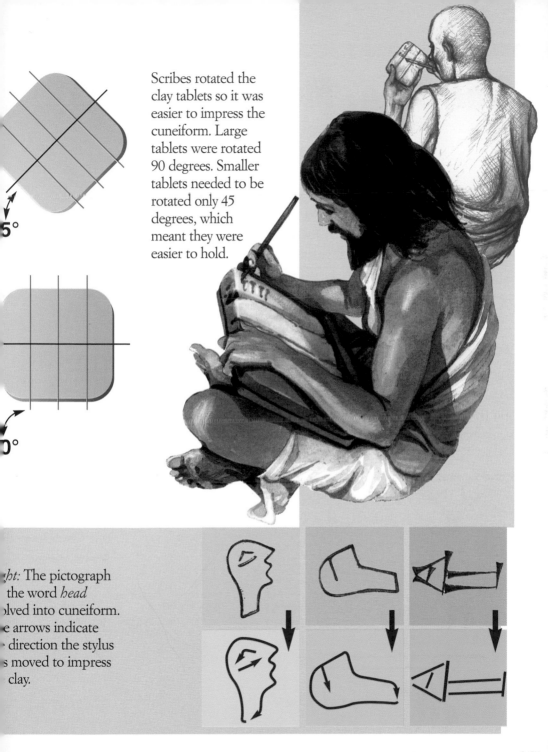

5°

0°

Scribes rotated the clay tablets so it was easier to impress the cuneiform. Large tablets were rotated 90 degrees. Smaller tablets needed to be rotated only 45 degrees, which meant they were easier to hold.

ght: The pictograph the word *head* olved into cuneiform. e arrows indicate direction the stylus s moved to impress clay.

One Sign, Many Meanings

At a certain point, Sumerian pictographs began to represent the sound of the word for an object as well as the object itself. Since many words had the same sound in the Sumerian language, a single sign could mean different things and a sign that represented one word could be used to write another that was pronounced the same way.

To distinguish them when read, classification signs were adopted. They were known as determinatives, which were written next to a pictograph to indicate whether the object or the sound was being represented.

Below: Few Sumeri signs indicated abstract concepts. This pictograph means "half."

first day

second day

third day

Left: The repetition of a sign increases i quantitative value.

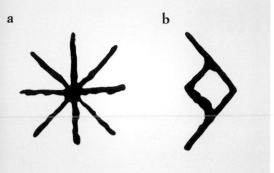

a   b

Top: When written in front of another symbol, the pictograph for star (a) indicates divinity. The pictograph for sun (b), when alone, represents the astronomical sun. When written as pictured, with "star" in front of "sun," the subject is the sun god.

Center: It would be difficult to represent the word *life* with an image, so Sumerians used the symbol for arrow to mean "life." The words *life* and *arrow* are both pronounced TI in Sumerian.

Bottom: The word *foot* is pronounced DU in Sumerian. Therefore, if the pictograph for foot is drawn twice, it is read as "dudu," which is also a proper name. The clay statue is of a scribe named Dudu who lived around 3350 BCE.

The Job of Writing

In a society in which few knew how to read and write, scribes were considered important people. Their work, though, was anything but easy. In addition to registering the offerings the faithful made to the temple and calculating the tributes due the sovereign, they drew up contracts for buying and selling, made wills and inventories, transcribed laws, and took care of diplomatic correspondence.

To become a scribe meant long, hard years of study that consisted mostly of copying model texts: lists of geographical names, names of birds and fish, grammar tables, mathematic texts, or measurement tables. Archaeologists have uncovered intact tablets with exercises and farmers' manuals.

Right: In Sumer, the scribes themselves prepared clay tablets. Scribes would write on the tablets while the clay was still moist and then dry them in the sun so that the marks could not be erased or changed.

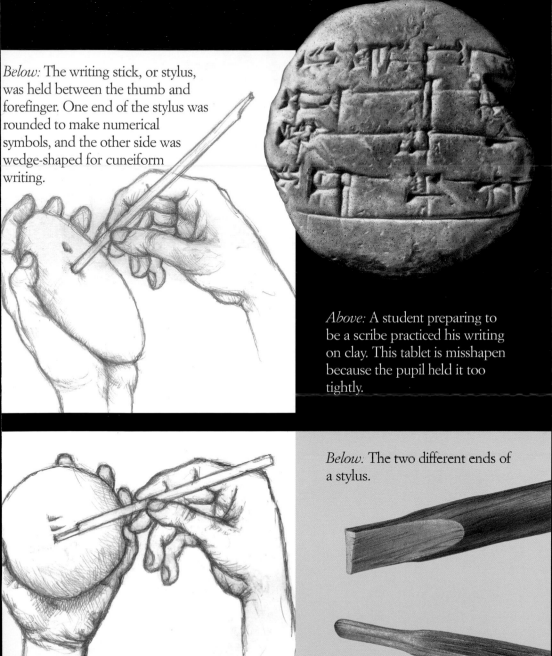

Below: The writing stick, or stylus, was held between the thumb and forefinger. One end of the stylus was rounded to make numerical symbols, and the other side was wedge-shaped for cuneiform writing.

Above: A student preparing to be a scribe practiced his writing on clay. This tablet is misshapen because the pupil held it too tightly.

Below. The two different ends of a stylus.

Books Made of Clay

In 1968 an Italian archaeologist discovered the city of Ebla in northern Syria, which yielded a rich, almost intact royal archive.

The archives consist of almost 2,000 whole tablets and over 15,000 large fragments covered with cuneiform writing on administrative and political subjects. But there are also legal, religious, and literary texts, as well as dictionaries (the first in history) and numerous foreign texts.

These documents allowed for the reconstruction of the history of Ebla—a rich, powerful kingdom with many tributary cities—and of the entire Near East in the 3rd millennium BCE.

Below, left: This tablet from Ebla has lists of cereals, oils, and livestock inscribed on it.

Opposite, top: An unusually shaped tablet from Ebla.

low: The Ebla tablets, clay books, were arranged and classified on ooden shelves according to subject, like a modern library, and trusted to numerous scribes.

Writing Grows Up

When Sumerian writing began to express the sounds of the spoken language, it was considered mature. It was then ready to transcribe religious hymns and lists of the kings, opening the way to the study of history. At the same time, epic literature began to flourish, such as the *Epic of Gilgamesh* (c. 2600 BCE). It is the story of the legendary king of Uruk and is the forerunner of the great legends of Greek mythology, particularly the feats of Hercules. It also tells of a universal flood surprisingly similar to the one in the Bible.

Above: Gilgamesh, the mythical hero of Sumerian literature Sumerian relief from the 8th century BCE

The first written codex, or book of laws, that has been discovered intact dates to the 18th century BCE. The laws, which were made by Babylonian king Hammurabi, were carved on stone so that they could be exhibited in the temples for all to see. It is known as the Code of Hammurabi.

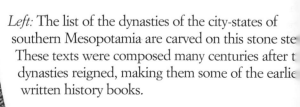

Left: The list of the dynasties of the city-states of southern Mesopotamia are carved on this stone stel These texts were composed many centuries after t dynasties reigned, making them some of the earlie written history books.

24

bove: The upper
rt of the Stele of
sa, a black basalt
one about 6 feet
m) high, on
hich the Code of
ammurabi is
graved. A relief of
ammurabi receiv-
g the law from the
n god Shamash
corates the base
the stele.

ght: Hammurabi
ctates his code to a
ibe. The code
nsists of 282 laws
garding violations,
mmerce, family,
operty, agriculture,
ges, rents, and
e sale and lending
slaves.

Cuneiform Conquers the Near East

Not surprisingly, Sumerian writing spread among the neighboring populations that spoke languages related to Sumerian, such as the Akkadians of northern Mesopotamia and the inhabitants of Elam (in present-day Iran).

But even the Hittites—who settled in Asia Minor around 2000 BCE and spoke a language that differed greatly from that of the Sumerians, Akkadians, or Elamites—adopted these cuneiform characters.

The Assyrians, who conquered the Near East beginning in 1300 BCE, used cuneiform characters to write the various languages of their empire. Cuneiform, therefore, became the oldest and most widespread method for written communication among the great civilizations of the Ancient Near East.

Right: This relief depicts two Assyrian scribes. One is writing on a tablet, the other on a papyrus scroll, a kind of paper made from reeds.

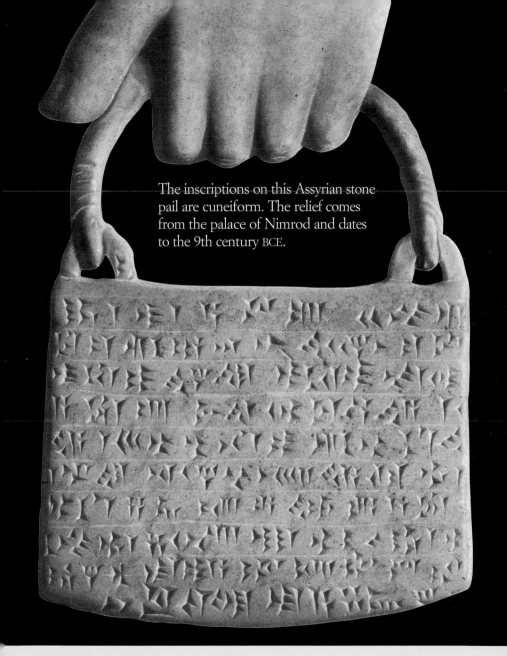

The inscriptions on this Assyrian stone pail are cuneiform. The relief comes from the palace of Nimrod and dates to the 9th century BCE.

Right: Cuneiform eventually developed to include five basic positions in which the wedge-shaped lines could be drawn: horizontal, two different diagonals, hooked, and vertical.

A Wedge-shaped Alphabet

In 1929, the writing used in the ancient port city of Ugarit (in present-day Syria) was discovered. Like cuneiform writing, Ugaritic script is made by digging the point of a sharp blade into a fresh clay tablet. The alphabet used in Ugarit transcribed a language that may have been an archaic form of Phoenician.

The Ugaritic script differed from the cuneiform writing of the Akkadians because it preserved only the sound of the initial consonant of a word or syllable, as if the Akkadian syllabic signs upon which it had been modeled had been split in two.

Opposite, top: The Ugaritic alphabet, which was deciphered in 1930, includes 30 signs and is the most complete of all the primitive alphabets.

Opposite, center: This tablet from Ugarit is inscribed with the oldest known alphabet.

Left: Ugaritic script was a simplification of Akkadian script. The Akkadian sign NA becomes N with the elimination of the vertical wedge and a different arrangement of the other wedges. PA is reduced to P.

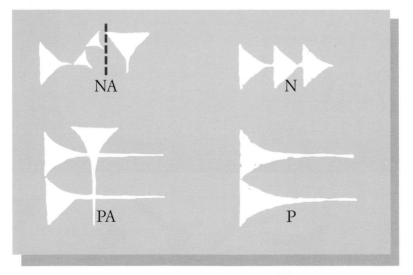

NA   N

PA   P

Ugaritic Alphabet

a	b	g	h	d	h	w	z	h.	t	y
k	s	l	m	s	n	z	s	'	p	s
q	r	t	ġ	ġ	t	í	u	ś		

Below: The ancient city of Ugarit, which flourished around 2000 BCE, was located on the coast of present-day Syria. Its ruins include a necropolis and a palace, where the tablets were found.

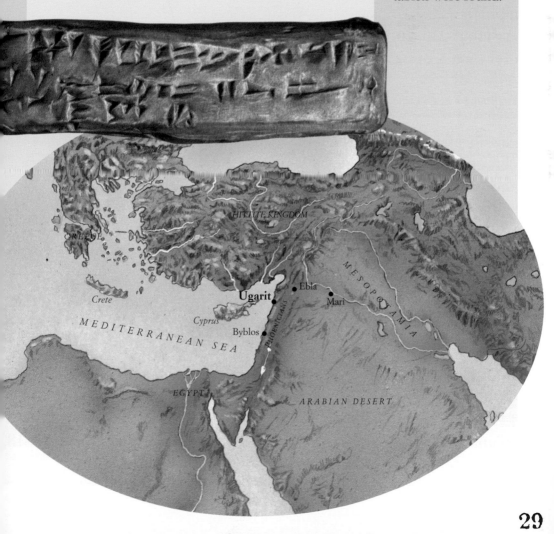

HITTITE KINGDOM

GREECE

Crete

Cyprus

MEDITERRANEAN SEA

Ugarit

Ebla

Mari

MESOPOTAMIA

Byblos

PHOENICIANS

EGYPT

ARABIAN DESERT

29

Index

Page numbers in **boldface** are illustrations, tables, and charts.